50 ÉTUDES FOR PIANO

NATASHA DEONARAIN

ASSURE PRESS

ASSURE PRESS

An imprint of Assure Press Publishing & Consulting, LLC

www.assurepress.org

Publisher's Note: Assure Press books may be purchased for educational, business, or sales promotional use. For information please visit the website.

50 Etudes for Piano/ Natasha Deonarain— 1st ed.

ISBN-13: 978-1-954573-02-4
eISBN-13: 978-1-954573-03-1
Library of Congress Control Number: 2021930010

for

elara, emma & sloane

may you always hear the music

CONTENTS

50 ÉTUDES FOR PIANO

étude 1

étude :
an attitude built in solitude, one note at a time

étude 2

one note   depressed   becomes agony
two notes   expressed   become harmony

étude 3

broken chords   are always connected &
                     long to be together

étude 4

musical notes can choose
      to be asynchronous
                  dissonant
          discordant
  or

they can choose
      to harmonize

           —trying to blame the piano—

étude 5 : rubik's cube

my	thought	your
love	turns into	sound
his	music	her

étude 6

music flows   like clouds
                 like rivers
                 like love
                          through your hands

étude 7

two notes

separate in pitch & quality
          one black
          one white

connect to each other
when a brass pedal

shaped like

half a heart is pressed
down to the floor

étude 8

let the scale
play for you

let your fingers
slip into a dip between
black & white

don't try
too hard—

when everything
else is gone
its music will

still play on

étude 9

when four hands
play a piano sometimes

they play together—
but most of the time

they drift apart

étude 10

pause: let yourself play anything you want
rest: let it all be forgiven

étude 11

a grand piano
          open—
placed in the center of a home
becomes its heart

étude 12

the same note
        played
        every day
cannot make
        a complete composition

étude 13

musical   notes
                    without
        arms   flags
              or   are
          to be continued...

étude 14

many black dots
can be joined together
by one or two or even three horizontal lines

or they can stand
alone

étude 15

when	how
will	will
you	the
question	treble
the bass	reply
?	?

—contrapuntal—

étude 16

why start
in the middle

why start
at C why not

A or B or G &
where does it go when
I lift my fingers

off the keys

étude 17 : angels & devils

a chromatic scale is played

    black then white then black &
    one half-step at a time with
    no history
    & no end

étude 18

see   : black, how it pulses inside these straight white veins &
         across the page
touch :   black & white fingers
feel   :   half of a   golden heart sink to the floor
hear :   chromatic gray tones
know :   the hunger that lurks inside

étude 19

confucious says:
                    "when soundboard cracks, you, audience
                              & pocketbook will suffer"

étude 20

the sound of pain   =   a cracked soundboard
the sound of music   =   a humidifier

    —self-care—

```
                    night     peace
            day                             love      sound
    day         day       sound     love       night      peace
night   day             night       peace     sound        love
    peace       night                  day
        sound         day     night       peace         love
        night       sound     day
                love       love      peace     night           day
        sound         day           night   love
                    peace
```

—busy-ness—

étude 22

we should all strive to put a black Yamaha piano
        in every child's home—

& of course,
world peace

étude 23

if you cannot hear | sit still
if you cannot see | & listen

    —I can't do it—

étude 24

instead of living inside a treehouse
& playing with dolls

she began to live inside
                    her piano
          & played there

—what a strange girl—

étude 25

when you go back to your mom's house
& walk into her living room;

you'll always find your old black Yamaha piano—
  & the same dip on her cloth-covered sofa

   —going home—

the number
of flats &
sharps passed
on
your way
to the stars
are like keys
on a piano

they'll always be there
when you
remember
to see

étude 27

why do we have to practice   ?
why work so hard   ?
why wish the practice hour away   ?

why can't we just play   ?

étude 28

did you
find
your
music
that wasn't
written
on the
page?

étude 29

        to practice every day
        learn all the rules—
               & then break   them

—advice for talented players—

étude 30

at the performance

      be ~~hear~~ ~~see~~ the pianist
      be ~~hear~~ ~~see~~ the audience
      be ~~hear~~ ~~see~~ the music

at the performance

étude 31

somewhere
there's
a girl
who takes piano
lessons

maybe
she's ten years old

by now

étude 32

she plays until
waterfalls

she plays until
skyfalls

she plays until she's

the only one
who listens—

the only one
who hears

étude 33 : elara's theme

three questions :
> what's the name of the composer ?
> what's the date of your recital ?
> what do you want more than anything in the world
> when you succeed ?

> —trying to get her to practice—

étude 34

sometimes   the sound
        comes from across the street

            behind closed doors where
                    I can no longer go—
                made by those
        I no longer know

but many times   it comes
        from inside the same room
                where I was before
what would I give   to listen once more

étude 35

pieces practiced & played
        unperfected

performance recitals
        unheard

conversations
        unfinished

all that we left for another day

étude 36

as she grows
there'll be other things
        to catch her eye—
there'll be other things
        to make her cry—

but as she grows
you won't have to try too hard—

for she'll always return
        to you

étude 37

basic instructions for piano players

   1) prop the lid
   2) open the fallboard
   3) adjust the bench
   4) place hands over the keyboard
   5) follow His cue

étude 38

your piano does not live—
                    —unless you are alive

étude 39 : for sloane

the relationship
         between composer & pianist is a heart
shaped like a piano

étude 40

composer: : takes music from her heart & puts it in her head
pianist: : takes music from his head & puts it in his heart
audience: : takes music from her ears & puts it in her soul

    —who are you—

étude 41

the difference between
       a major & a minor

              lies strictly in how you scale
              your attitude

étude 42

the one who listens will make all the decisions
— for the one who performs—

étude 43

the music may stop　　:　　for months or years
but it will always　　　:　　begin again

　　　　—where did you let it go—

étude 44

      how big was the gift you got
           —what did you get—
           —how much did it cost—

&
how big was the one you gave away

étude 45

always
sit on the bench dressed in your
sunday best—
        inside & out

étude 46

> ma chérie
> tu dois chercher
> tous les jours de ta vie
> trouves ta compositrice
> puis n'as jamais lâcher
> .

> my dear
> you must search
> all the days of your life
> find your composer
> & then never let go

—what I wish for you—

étude 47: for emma

the song doesn't come from inside
your piano—
it comes from inside
you

étude 48

when you have this music—
         —the world can never be a lonely place

étude 49

one finger pressed to
     one key
         ‖ : will make you sin(k) : ‖

all fingers pressed to
     all keys
         ‖ : will make you sin(g) : ‖

—choose a different ending—

étude 50

seasons turned
     sound tumbled
          over & onto itself
     around & around

          disappearing from one place
            & into the next

ABOUT THE AUTHOR

Natasha Deonarain is the recipient of the 2020 Three Sisters Award by *NELLE magazine* and has been featured in *Little Red Tree International Poetry Prize Anthology* (2012). Her work appears in *The Inflectionist Review, Rogue Agent Journal, The RavensPerch, Connecticut Review*, and *Door is Ajar* among others. She lives in Arizona, depending on weather patterns, and sometimes practices medicine.